SCI-FI TECH

WHAT WOULD IT TAKE TO
UPLOAD A MIND?

BY MEGAN RAY DURKIN

CAPSTONE PRESS
a capstone imprint

Capstone Captivate is published by Capstone Press, an imprint of Capstone.
1710 Roe Crest Drive
North Mankato, Minnesota 56003
www.capstonepub.com

Library of Congress Cataloging-in-Publication Data
Names: Durkin, Megan Ray, author.
Title: What would it take to upload a mind? / by Megan Ray Durkin.
Description: North Mankato, Minnesota : [Capstone Press], [2020] | Series:
  Sci-fi tech | Includes index. | Audience: Grades: 4-6
Identifiers: LCCN 2019029522 (print) | LCCN 2019029523 (ebook) | ISBN
  9781543591194 (hardcover) | ISBN 9781496665997 (paperback) | ISBN 9781543591279 (ebook)
Subjects: LCSH: Whole brain emulation--Juvenile literature |
  Brain--Juvenile literature. | Uploading of data--Juvenile literature. |
  Neurotechnology (Bioengineering)--Juvenile literature.
Classification: LCC TA167.5 .D87 2020 (print) | LCC TA167.5 (ebook) | DDC 620.8/2--dc23
LC record available at https://lccn.loc.gov/2019029522
LC ebook record available at https://lccn.loc.gov/2019029523

Image Credits
Getty Images: AFP, 19, Mark Boster/Los Angeles Times, 14; iStockphoto: Just_Super, cover, metamorworks, 29; Oak Ridge National Laboratory: Carlos Jones, 13; Science Source: James King-Holmes, 16; Shutterstock Images: adike, 12, Epstock, 11, F.Neidl, 15, Gorodenkoff, 20, Gorodenkoff, 24, Gorodenkoff, 25, Kateryna Kon, 21, Marina Pousheva, 28, Maxim Gaigul, 23, Rost9, 6, Sebastian Kaulitzki, 5, sfam_photo, 10, Skorzewiak, 26–27, Tefi, 9
Design Elements: Shutterstock Images

Editorial Credits
Editor: Arnold Ringstad; Designer: Laura Graphenteen

Printed in the United States of America.
PA99

TABLE OF CONTENTS

WORDS IN BOLD ARE IN THE GLOSSARY.

CHAPTER ONE

FROM YOUR BRAIN TO A COMPUTER

What weighs 3 pounds (1.4 kilograms) and sits in your head? It's your brain! The brain has many parts. They must work together perfectly. The brain controls all of what we do. It controls your breathing. It controls movement. Your brain lets you know what is happening around you.

The brain makes our thoughts. Together, all of these thoughts are called the mind. Could we **upload** the mind? This would mean copying the mind and storing it on a computer. Scientists are trying to answer this question. Some believe the brain has too many parts for this to work. But others think it is possible. Maybe our minds could live longer than our bodies. Could minds even live forever on a computer?

The brain gives us our thoughts and feelings.

Many nerve cells are packed into the brain.

CHAPTER TWO

WHAT DOES IT MEAN TO UPLOAD A MIND?

The brain is an **organ**. Organs are parts of the body that have jobs. One of the brain's jobs is to make thoughts. Together, a person's thoughts are the mind. But how does a brain make those thoughts?

Cells are the smallest parts that make up a living thing. Different organs have different kinds of cells. The brain is made up of billions of **nerve cells**. The brain's nerve cells send messages to each other. These messages make thoughts. The cells are always sending messages. They make new thoughts all the time.

FUN FACT

There are nerve cells outside the brain too. The longest one stretches from the hips to the feet.

To upload a mind, scientists need to figure out where all of the brain's nerve cells are. This job is hard. There are about 100 billion of these cells in a brain. Scientists would need to **scan** the brain. A scan is a picture of something inside the body. The scan would need to show where all the cells are. The scanner would have to send this information to a computer.

The next part is even harder. A mind is more than a picture of where cells are. It is made of thoughts. Those are made when cells send messages. So scientists would also need to figure out the messages the cells send. They would need to know where each message goes. They would need to know when the cells send each message.

FUN FACT

The brain uses about as much energy as a small light bulb.

NERVE CELL CONNECTIONS

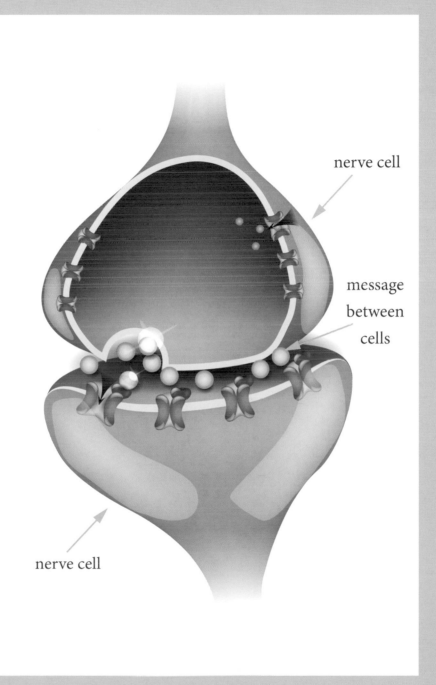

nerve cell

message between cells

nerve cell

CHAPTER THREE

HOW WOULD MIND UPLOADING WORK?

The first step in uploading a mind is scanning the brain. Scientists need pictures of the brain. They need to see where every nerve cell is. They also need to see how the cells connect.

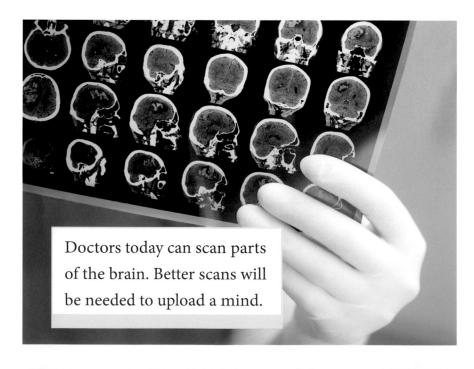

Doctors today can scan parts of the brain. Better scans will be needed to upload a mind.

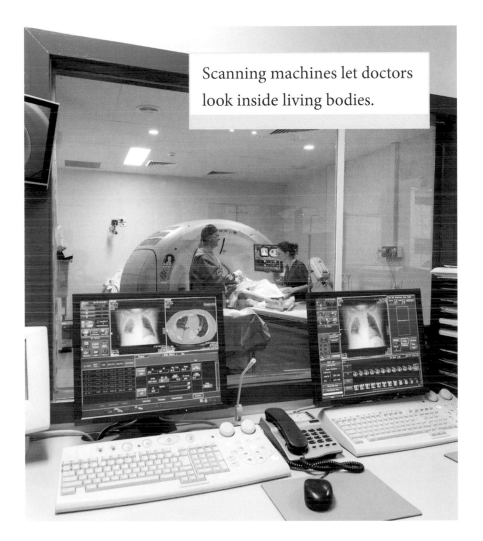

Scanning machines let doctors look inside living bodies.

The scanning machine would send this information to a computer **program**. A program is a set of instructions that a computer follows. First the program would store the information. It would know where each cell is in the brain.

Next the program would copy the brain's activity. Everything that happens in a real brain would happen in the program. Each nerve cell connects to about 8,000 others. The program would need to make all these connections. It would have to send the right messages at the right times.

What would happen next? Scientists are not sure. Would the uploaded mind make thoughts? Could the program itself have feelings? Scientists are thinking about how to answer these questions.

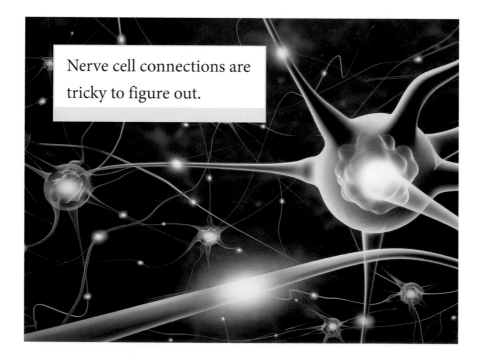

Nerve cell connections are tricky to figure out.

Mind uploading would need powerful computers. Today's most powerful computers take up whole rooms.

The brains of lab animals are sliced thinly before they are studied.

CHAPTER FOUR

CURRENT TECH

Scientists study animals to learn more about how brains work. They have figured out where the nerve cells are in some animal brains. Scientists have done this for a worm brain. They have done it for a mouse brain too. The scientists looked at parts of the brain. They figured out how the cells connected.

Worms have very simple brains.

Scientists studied the worm to figure out how its nerve cells work.

Scientists tried simple mind uploading using the worm brain. The worm has only about 300 nerve cells. This makes figuring out how its brain works an easier job. Scientists used a computer program to build a copy of the brain. Then they uploaded the program to a toy robot.

The robot acted like the worm. It moved forward or backward when touched. It was not a perfect test. Scientists could not make an exact copy of the worm brain. But the test is one step on the way to uploading a mind. Scientists are learning how to do the same thing with bigger brains.

STUDYING THE HUMAN BRAIN

A worm brain is simple. The human brain is much larger. Figuring out where all its nerve cells are is a hard job. The U.S. government is spending money to do it. It has spent tens of millions of dollars. More than 100 scientists are working on this.

Scientists worked with mice too. They used mice with special **genes**. How a living thing looks and acts depends on its genes. The special genes colored the mice's nerve cells. Ninety different colors were shown. Scientists called this the Brainbow. This word is a mix of "brain" and "rainbow."

The Brainbow looks cool. But it's also useful for learning how the brain works. Before, scientists could use genes to give nerve cells two colors. The Brainbow has many colors. This makes it easier to see how cells connect. It is a step closer to figuring out how the brain works.

The Brainbow helped scientists learn how brains work.

Scientists will need to create a machine that can scan the brain without harming its owner.

CHAPTER FIVE

WHAT TECH IS NEEDED?

Scientists today cannot upload a human mind. Scanners are not good enough. They can scan only small pieces of brain. Scanning a whole brain is much harder.

Very tiny machines might help. These machines could move through the body. They could go into the brain. They could figure out where all the nerve cells are. Then they could send that information to a computer.

Tiny machines might help with mind uploading someday.

To upload a mind, powerful computers would be needed. A brain has many parts. It would take up a lot of computer storage space. Imagine a piece of brain about the size of a grain of sugar. The **data** in that tiny piece could fill hundreds of computers! Data is information stored by computers. The brain contains a lot of data.

EYEWIRE

Scientists made a game called *EyeWire*. People can go online to play. The game is about connecting nerve cells. It is like solving a puzzle. But it helps scientists figure out how cells really connect. More than 200,000 people have played. People under 13 years old must get permission from a parent or guardian to try *EyeWire*.

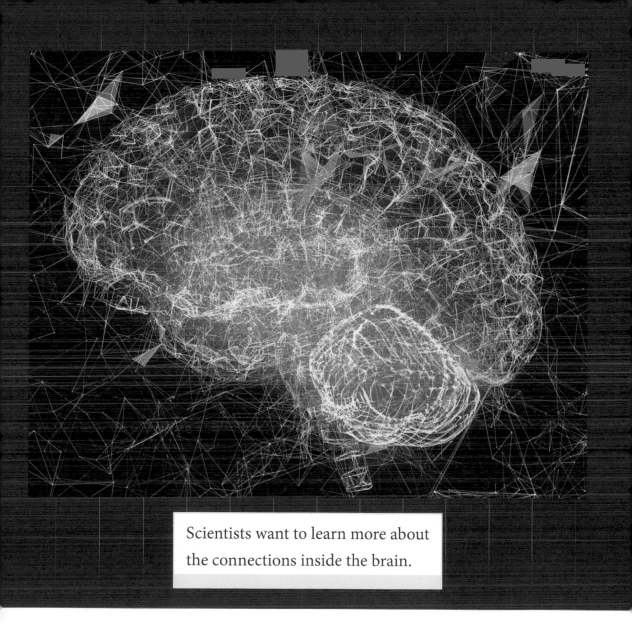

Scientists want to learn more about the connections inside the brain.

Storing data is just the first step. Then the information must be studied. Computer programs can look at the information. They can see pictures of the nerve cells. They can figure out how those cells connect.

Future scientists may explore uploaded human brains in virtual reality.

CHAPTER SIX

WHAT COULD THE FUTURE LOOK LIKE?

When a person dies, the brain stops working. Nerve cells stop sending signals. The mind no longer exists. Could uploading a mind let a person's brain live on? Could the mind continue to make new memories and thoughts? Could it even live forever? A mind in a computer would not need food. It would not need water. It would not grow old. It would just need power to run the computer.

Uploading a mind could make new things possible.

Imagine a woman gets her mind uploaded. Scientists hook her up to the uploading machine. She goes to sleep. What happens next? Perhaps when she wakes up, a copy of her mind is in the computer. She wakes up in her body and continues her life. But the copy of her mind lives on forever in the computer.

FUN FACT

Science-fiction movies show what life could be like in the future. The idea of mind uploading has been featured in many science-fiction movies.

Someday a human mind might be uploaded to a spacecraft. Then it could explore space.

Uploading a mind could have scientific uses. Traveling through space takes a long time. Going to faraway planets could take thousands of years. But humans live only around 100 years. Human minds could be uploaded into the computer on a spacecraft. They could learn about the universe. They could send what they learned back to Earth.

The human brain is amazing. It has billions of parts that work together. Uploading a brain may seem hard today. But science has solved many problems that once seemed hard. Scientists are learning more about the brain every day. Technology is getting better and better. Someday uploading a mind could be possible!

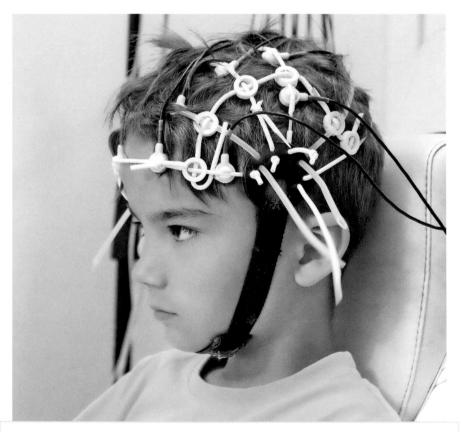

Today's doctors have ways to study brain activity. This technology will need to advance to make mind uploading real.

Scientists hope to fully understand the brain and how it works.

GLOSSARY

cell (SELL)—the smallest part that makes up a living thing

data (DAY-tuh)—information stored on a computer

gene (JEEN)—a set of chemicals found in the body that tells how a living thing will look

nerve cell (NURV sell)—a kind of cell in the body that sends messages to other cells

organ (OR-gin)—a part of the body that has its own jobs

program (PRO-gram)—a set of instructions that a computer follows

scan (SKAN)—a picture of something inside the body

upload (UP-lode)—to send something to a computer

READ MORE

Martin, Claudia. *Computers*. Mankato, Minn.: Capstone Press, 2019.

Meister, Cari. *Totally Wacky Facts about the Mind*. Mankato, Minn.: Capstone Press, 2016.

Swanson, Jennifer. *Brain Games: The Mind-Blowing Science of Your Amazing Brain*. Washington, D.C.: National Geographic Kids, 2015.

INTERNET SITES

How Does Your Brain Work?
http://whoami.sciencemuseum.org.uk/whoami/findoutmore/yourbrain/howdoesyourbrainwork

Nat Geo Kids: Your Amazing Brain
https://www.natgeokids.com/za/discover/science/general-science/human-brain/

Neuroscience for Kids: Experiments and Activities
https://faculty.washington.edu/chudler/experi.html

INDEX